Living a Good Life

Advice on Virtue, Love, and Action from the Ancient Greek Masters

Translated from the Arabic
by Thomas Cleary

SHAMBHALA
Boston & London
1997

SHAMBHALA PUBLICATIONS, INC.
HORTICULTURAL HALL
300 MASSACHUSETTS AVENUE
BOSTON, MA 02115
http://www.shambhala.com

9 8 7 6 5 4 3 2 1

First Edition

Printed in Canada

♾ This edition is printed on acid-free paper that meets the
American National Standards Institute Z39.48

Distributed in the United States by Random House, Inc. and in Canada
by Random House of Canada Ltd

Library of Congress Cataloging-in-Publication Data
Living a good life: advice on virtue, love, and action from the ancient Greek
masters/translated from the Arabic by Thomas Cleary.—1st ed.
p. cm.
Includes bibliographical references (p.   )
ISBN 1-57062-274-4 (alk. paper)
1. Conduct of life.   2. Ethics, Ancient.   I. Cleary, Thomas F., 1949–
  BJ1595.L75   1997   96-44398
  170'.44—dc21   CIP

Contents

Introduction

GRECIAN CULTURE AND THOUGHT are universally acknowledged to be among the main roots of Western civilization, and the inspiration of the European Renaissance. Grecian cultures and philosophies were originally of considerable variety and were also commingled with other cultures and ways of thought, including the already ancient as well as the contemporarily current. Elements of Minoan, Egyptian, Chaldean, Indian, Persian, and Hebrew cultures were absorbed by inquisitive Greek peoples over the centuries, producing dynamic new syntheses.

The Greek empire declined in time, superceded in the West by the Romans, but the high culture of the Graeco-Roman synthesis remained essentially Greek in many important ways. When the center of Roman culture was destroyed by Teutonic tribes, therefore, both Latin and Greek literature and culture faded in the Western part of the former empire. The antagonism of the Roman Church to the Greek accelerated the disappearance of Greek scholarship from Western Europe.

It was not until the twelfth century, seven hundred years after the sack of Rome, that the rendering of Greek classics into Latin got underway on a broad scale for wider use in Western Europe. They were not translated only from the original Greek at that time, however, but also from classical Arabic versions. By the twelfth century, under the impact of Saracen culture in Spain and Italy, Arabic had largely superceded Latin as the dominant learned language of continental Western Europe. The process of transferring Graeco-Arabic learning into the domain of Latin Christendom in preparation for the Renaissance was just beginning.

The Arabic versions of Greek classics had been made several hundred years earlier. This translation work reached its peak in the eighth and ninth centuries under the patronage of the Abbasid Caliphate. This massive endeavor was part of a major new Islamic cultural synthesis embodying the sayings of the Prophet Muhammad, "Seeking knowledge is encumbent upon every Muslim," and "Seek the word of wisdom, wherever it may be found."

The Abbasids were descendants of the Quraish, an aristocratic clan of hereditary shrine keepers of Mecca in olden times. The Quraish were well known for collecting information and artifacts of the religions and beliefs of the peoples of other lands with whom they engaged in trade. Muhammad the Prophet, who is said to have welcomed wise men from the East, was himself a member of the Quraish clan. Up until the zenith of its empire, the Abbasid Caliphate drew its top ministers from the Barmakis, a family of hereditary Buddhist priests and shrine keepers in what is now Afghanistan.

By the twelfth century, when Arabic versions of Greek classics were translated into Latin under Saracen influence, many studies and commentaries on Greek classics had been composed by Persians writing in Arabic. Jewish scholars and philosophers also used the Arabic language, not only for studies of Greek thinking, but even for Hebrew grammar and Biblical interpretation. Arabic schools in Saracen Spain attracted Christians, Jews, and Muslims. Interested in science, religion, mysticism, and philosophy, people of all three faiths worked side-by-side, revitalizing civilization in Western Europe.

After the rendition of Greek classics into Arabic, the challenge of Greek rationalism to Islamic pragmatism was answered, both theologically and mystically, by certain Sufis who demonstrated the compatibility of reason and religion. Astronomy, mathematics, medicine, and other natural sciences were consequently developed to a high degree by Sufis and other Islamic workers. Influences of this new cultural synthesis extended through most of Western Europe, in time affecting education and literature as far away as England.

Abstract theology and natural science thus made great strides under the impact of Graeco-Arabic learning, stimulating the revival and enrichment of the Western consciousness. Among the diverse communities of ordinary people within Saracenic culture, meanwhile, aphoristic literature from the Greek sources gained particularly great popularity. Rendered in simple, clear Arabic, concerned only with practical content and meaning rather than literary embellishment and philosophical speculation, collections of wise sayings attributed to Greek ancients became the most widespread vehicle of popular Graeco-Arabic culture.

The present volume is a collection of translations from these popular Arabic versions of Greek wisdom lore. It is presented in five parts. The first part consists of sayings attributed to a variety of ancient philosophers, including Pythagoras, Diogenes, and Hermes, as well as Socrates, Plato, and Aristotle. These are arranged according to topic. The second part consists entirely of sayings attributed to Plato; the third part of sayings attributed to his disciple Aristotle. The fourth part is a collection of Neo-Platonic meditations whose Arabic attribution is simply "The Greek Master."

The fifth part of this volume contains parallel selections from other wisdom literature of the world, including Taoist, Confucian, Buddhist, and Islamic. This last section is included to illustrate something of the commonality of human concerns in an extended global context, much as the Graeco-Arabic wisdom literature appealed to the widely recognized heritage of Greek civilization as a means of connecting Jewish, Christian, and Islamic sensibilities in a community of common conscience and consciousness.

Part One

Aphorisms of the Masters

Money

1

One day money was mentioned in the presence of Pythagoras. He remarked, "What do I need with something that is given by fortune and luck, preserved by meanness and stinginess, and annihilated by generosity and liberality?"

2

Socrates said, "The intellectual is a doctor of faith, and money is a sickness thereof; so when you see the doctor bringing the sickness on himself, how can he treat anyone else?"

3

Plato said, "The wealthy one is not the one who amasses money, but the one who manages it well and knows how to save and to spend."

4

When told that a certain person was rich, Diogenes said, "I would not know that until I knew how he manages his money."

5

Aristotle said, "Let your interest in seeking wealth be graciousness to friends."

6

Plato said, "A miser is as ready to give up his honor and dignity as he is eager to keep his money; a generous man is as intent on keeping his honor and dignity as he is open-handed with his money."

7

Told of a man who had a lot of money, Diogenes said, "I wouldn't be happy for him without knowing that he used his money well."

8

A king presented Pythagoras with a gift, but the philosopher returned it to him. When the king questioned him about it, Pythagoras said, "It was because of the fact that the giving of what is there and the seeking of what is wanting are from richness or poverty of soul. Thus I did not want you to be generous to my greediness or for you to be enriched at the price of my impoverishment."

9

Pythagoras said, "Love of money is the beginning of evil, because the operation of evil is connected to love of money."

Children

1

Pythagoras was told, "Had you married, a child would have been born to you that would have made you happy."

The philosopher retorted, "It is out of my love for children that I have given up seeking to have children."

2

Socrates was asked, "Why do you always associate with the young?"

He replied, "I do it as horse trainers do; for they look to train young colts, not old nags."

3

Socrates said, "How ugly are the decorations of decorators, though they imitate beautiful form! Yet sons neglect to emulate their worthy fathers!"

4

Plato said, "Don't force your children into your ways, for they were created for a time different from your time."

5

Socrates was asked, "What use is education to the young?"

He replied, "If they get nothing more from it than that it restrains them from bad habits, that is enough."

6

Plato said, "It behooves those who take the young to task to leave them room for excuse, lest they drive them to be hardened by too much rebuke."

Politicians and Philosophers

1

The corrupt dictator of Sicily asked Pythagoras to stay with him, but the philosopher said to the dictator, "Your intelligence is lost, at odds with what would profit you; your constitution is agitated, uprooting your foundation. So do not try to get me to stay with you, for it is not a condition of healers to be ill along with the ailing!"

2

When Socrates was asked why he didn't visit the king, he said, "Why should I?"

He was told, "He is our master, and we are his servants; so whoever is closer to him is superior to whoever is more remote."

Socrates retorted, "But he is enslaved to what I have mastered, and he is ruled by what I rule."

This anecdote was reported to the king, who summoned Socrates and said to him, "I hear you said I am enslaved to what you have mastered, and ruled by what you rule. What are you referring to?"

Socrates said, "The passions. They are your rulers, while I rule them; they are my servants, while you are their slaves!"

The king exclaimed, "You have spoken truly! Well said, by God! Do you want some money?"

Socrates replied, "By God, I do not have any place to store even a coin, let alone anything else. And what would I do with money?"

He was told, "It will be useful to you in this world."

Socrates said, "And it will hurt my afterlife, distracting me from purity of obedience and making me fearful and scared, making me responsible for guarding it, and complicating my routine."

3

When Alexander asked Aristotle to go with him to the lands of Asia, Aristotle said, "I don't want to impose slavery on myself when I am free."

4

It was related that Socrates used to sun himself on top of the barrel in which he used to take shelter. The king stopped by and said to him, "Hey Socrates! What hinders you from coming to us?"

Socrates replied, "Preoccupation with what sustains life."

The king said, "If you came to us, we would have met your requirements in that regard," assuming that Socrates meant livelihood, whereas he had meant life everlasting.

Anyway, Socrates said, "Had I found that with you, I would have stayed with you as long as the need for it stayed with me."

So the king said to him, "Ask for what you need."

Socrates responded, "My need is for you to remove your shadow from me, for you have been interfering with my enjoyment of the sunshine."

Then the king called for sumptuous clothing of silk brocade and other materials, and gold and jewels, to be given to Socrates. But Socrates said, "O king, you have promised that which sustains life, but you are offering that which sustains death. Socrates has no need of stones from the earth, or the stalks of plants, or the spittle of caterpillars. What Socrates needs is with him wherever he bends his steps."

5

When he left the presence of a king, Pythagoras was asked what the king was doing. The philosopher replied, "He is impoverishing the people."

6

Plato said, "Intoxication is forbidden to the ruler, because he is the protector of the state, and it is disgraceful that the protector be in need of someone to watch out for him."

7

Alexander said to Aristotle, "Advise me, since you are not going along with me."

So Aristotle told him, "Make your deliberateness the

bridle of your hurry, make your strategy the emissary of your force, and make your pardon the basis of your power; then I guarantee you the hearts of your subjects, as long as you don't oppress them by violence against them or make them reckless by pampering them."

8

It was said that when Alexander conquered a certain city he put its inhabitants to the sword after winning victory over them. So Aristotle wrote to him, "You were mistaken in doing this, because those people were your enemies in war, but when you conquered them they became your servants; and it is vile for a man to mistreat his servants. So in victory it behooves one to lay down the weapons of wrath with the weapons of warfare."

9

Alexander told Diogenes that he himself was the greatest king. Diogenes said, "I am Diogenes the Cynic; I fawn on the good and the virtuous, and I bark at and bite those who are different from that."

Alexander asked Diogenes, "Do you fear me?"

Diogenes asked back, "Are you good or bad?"

Alexander said, "Good."

Diogenes said, "I do not fear, but rather love, one who is good."

10

Alexander went to a certain place to make war on its people, but the women fought back against him, so he desisted and refrained from fighting them, saying, "If we overcome this army, there is no honor in it for us; and if we are overcome, it will be an enduring shame."

Wisdom

1

Asked about wisdom, Pythagoras called it "Knowledge of the realities of things existing in a single state eternally."

2

Aristotle's teacher, Plato, asked him, "What is the proof confirming God Most High?"

Aristotle said, "Nothing of God's creation gives more cogent proof of God than anything else."

3

Plato said, "The business of a philosopher is to know the essences of things, not their superficials."

4

Aristotle said, "Whoever wants to see the form of his naked soul should make wisdom his mirror."

5

Pythagoras said, "Wisdom is the medicine of souls."

6

Aristotle said, "I used to drink yet increase in thirst, until I knew the Truth, sublime Its splendor; then my thirst was quenched without drinking."

7

Plato used to pace when he wanted to teach, in deference to wisdom. And he used to say, "Call upon the self to serve wisdom, not sitting down in disrespect toward it."

He also said, "The specialty of wisdom is the comprehension of what is knowable. And along with comprehension of what is knowable, it is the purification of the soul. And along with its purification of the soul, it makes its possessor like the Primary Cause, in that the purpose of wisdom is to grace human souls and repel depravities from them."

8

Pythagoras said, "Fathers are the cause of life, but the wise are the cause of wholesome life."

9

Aristotle was the mentor and teacher of Alexander the Great. Alexander's esteem for him reached the point where he was asked whether he had more love for his mentor or his father. Alexander said, "My mentor, because my father was the proximate cause of my being, whereas my mentor, Aristotle, was a cause of bettering my being."

It is also reported that Alexander said, "My father was the cause of my temporal existence, whereas Aristotle was the cause of my eternal life."

10

Aristotle said, "Desire for intelligence is better than desire for wealth."

11

Plato said, "Among the things that facilitate an individual's search for wisdom is help from luck. And by "luck" I do not mean that whereof the cause is unknown, but rather divine fortune, which illumines the intelligence and guides it to the realities of things."

Then Plato was questioned about the influence of this luck. He replied, "It is not of one sort only, for the following reason. When one senses a light by which one's intelligence is illumined, whether one is awake or asleep, let one observe: One who sees no shape or form to the light, but just a simple radiance, should know that it is the divine light. If one sees it in a projected human form, but not that of a recognizable person, one should know it is the light of the intelligence. If one sees it in the form of a recognizable person, one should know it is the light of the self."

Change

1

Pythagoras said, "The world is a series of changes, sometimes in your favor and sometimes against you: so when you are in charge, do good; and when you are overruled, bear it."

2

Seeing an old man who wanted to take up philosophy but was embarrassed, Socrates said to him, "Don't be embarrassed to become better at the end of your life than you were to begin with."

3

Socrates said, "We ought to be distressed at life and happy to die, because we live to die and we die to live."

The Human Soul

1

Pythagoras wanted to admonish the people and censure them for their neglect of knowledge, so he climbed up onto a high place and cried, "O community of people!" Then when they had gathered, Pythagoras said, "I didn't call *you* —I only called *people!*"

2

Pythagoras said, "It is impossible for anything of the noble, lofty divine sciences to be firmly rooted in a soul while it is filled with squalor, since like appeals only to like."

3

Plato said, "The superior soul is beyond joy and does not sorrow. That is because joy only occurs when the good aspects of something are seen, and not the bad; and sorrow is on account of seeing the bad aspects of something and not the good. But the superior soul considers something in terms of what it leads to, what it offers, and what its liabilities are; and since the virtues and defects thereof balance each other as far as the superior soul is concerned, neither condition of joy or sorrow overcomes it."

4

Aristotle said, "There are four excellences of the soul, with four equivalent excellences of the body.

"Wisdom in the soul has its physical equivalent in perfection.

"Justice in the soul has its physical equivalent in beauty.

"Courage in the soul has its physical equivalent in strength.

"Modesty in the soul has its physical equivalent in health."

5

Pythagoras often used to say that it is fitting for a man to have a good build in youth, to be chaste while growing up, to be upright as a young man, to be perspicacious in maturity, and to be a keeper of norms in old age and at the time of death, so that regret does not overtake him after he dies.

6

Aristotle said, "Let your concern be with exercise of the soul. As for exercise of the body, take an interest in it to the degree that necessity calls for it; and flee pleasures, for they drain weak souls, though they have no power over the strong."

7

Plato said, "If anyone is melancholy, let him listen to the melodies of the noble soul. For the light of the soul dies out when melancholy enters it, while the light of the soul blazes when it is happy and rejoices. Melancholy appears according to longing, to the extent that the one subject to it admits it; and the susceptibility of the one subject to it corresponds to one's purity and innocence of dishonesty and pollution."

8

Aristotle said, "The soul is not within the body; rather, the body is within the soul, because the soul is more extensive than the body, and greater in magnitude."

Law

1

Pythagoras said, "Hold yourselves to three things from the law: abandon anger and importunity, avoid overconsumption, and do not sleep excessively."

2

Seeing him in a garment so threadbare that it did not cover him completely, a man exclaimed in amazement, "This is Socrates, lawgiver of the Athenians?"

Socrates retorted, "New clothes are not the sign of true law, nor are worn clothes the sign of false law."

3

Socrates said, "One who is benevolent by nature adheres to the law."

4

Socrates said, "Just as it is by physicians that the sick are purged and restored, so it is by laws that the unjust are reformed."

Self-Destruction

1

Pythagoras said, "The water that gags is sweet, the bread that chokes is delicious; and therein lies the destruction of people's devices."

2

Plato said, "Lust is a powerful snare for falling into evil."

3

Pythagoras was asked, "What is passion?"

He said, "Folly that has occurred to, or happened upon, an idle heart."

4

Plato said, "Don't plant a date palm inside your house."

Modesty

1

Pythagoras said, "If you want your life to be pleasant, be content to be thought of as ignorant."

2

Socrates said, "If he who knows not would simply remain silent, disputation would stop."

3

Pythagoras said, "Don't brag about what you did today, for you don't know what tomorrow will bring."

4

Socrates used to study music in his old age. He was asked, "Aren't you embarrassed to be studying in spite of your old age?"

Socrates replied, "I would be more embarrassed to be ignorant in spite of my age!"

5

Plato said, "If not for the fact that in my saying that I don't know is confirmation that I do know, I would have said I don't know."

6

Aristotle said, "If I am ignorant and I know I am ignorant, that is to me preferable to being ignorant and ignorant of my ignorance."

7

Seeing a woman all dressed up for a trip to the city, Socrates remarked, "I suspect that your trip is not to see the city, but for the city to see you."

Virtue and Action

1

Pythagoras said, "It is not enough for virtue to exist in the soul without emerging into action by effort. And effort is in training, by means of study, the irascible part of the self that is not submissive to order, so that the self may acquire education, skill, and aspiration for what is best."

2

When Socrates was asked about the virtuous man, he said, "The virtuous man at the highest level is the one who strives for virtues of his own accord. The virtuous man at the secondary level is the one who is motivated toward virtues when he hears of them from another. As for one who neglects both imperatives, he is vile and depraved."

3

Pythagoras said, "Ignorance of virtues is equivalent to death."

4

Plato said, "The good are those for whom undertaking the benefit of people is easier than undertaking their harm."

5

Irritated by an imbecile who had stopped Socrates and was annoying him, one of his friends said to the philosopher, "Permit me to restrain him."

Socrates replied, "One who permits malice is not a man of wisdom."

6

Plato said, "How hard it is for the covetous one to become virtuous!"

7

Pythagoras said, "Don't even entertain the notion of something that is not right to do."

8

Aristotle went to visit Plato and saw that he was angry. Aristotle inquired, "What has angered you, Teacher?"

Plato replied, "Something about you, of which a trustworthy individual has informed me."

Aristotle said, "A trustworthy individual does not slander."

Plato's anger then ceased.

9

Socrates said, "The error in giving to the undeserving is the same as withholding from the deserving."

Appearance and Reality

1

Pythagoras said, "One whose face is comely but whose morals are bad is like a vessel that is of gold but has vinegar in it."

2

Seeing a man with a handsome face whose behavior was bad, Diogenes said, "The house is nice, but the resident is a devil."

3

Men and women used to gather around Socrates to learn wisdom. One day he saw a young student of his fixing his gaze on the face of a woman named Hipparchia, who had a beautiful appearance and was a philosopher. Now Socrates said to himself, "Maybe this youth is distracted at heart and his glance fell on this woman's face while his soul was preoccupied with thought about something else."

Now this young man was of high rank, so Socrates let the matter rest until he realized that he was gazing at her intentionally. Then Socrates said, "Young man, what is this ugly look that has appeared from you, and this pre-occupaton that has hindered you from reflection and meditation?"

As if excusing himself, the young man said, "I marvel

at the beauty of the effects on her form of the wisdom of nature!"

But Socrates said, "No, my son. Don't make the beauty of the representation of individualities a vehicle for desires, lest you be carried away by them into a sticky morass. And it is for you to notice that gazing at Hipparchia's outward form blots out your vision, whereas gazing at her inner form will sharpen your vision."

4

When a picture of Socrates was shown to a man who claimed to be a physiognomist, he said, "This is a man overcome by corrupt desire."

People laughed at him and said, "This is Socrates, the most abstinent of people!"

But Socrates said to them, "Don't be hasty, for the man did not lie. I am by disposition guilty of what he said, but I master my self and subjugate my desire."

5

Noticing two men who were virtually inseparable, Pythagoras asked what kinship there was between them. He was told, "They are not related, but they are the best of friends."

Pythagoras remarked, "If that were so, then one wouldn't be rich while the other is poor!"

6

It was related that a sophist said to Socrates, "How ugly your figure is!"

Socrates replied, "Your comeliness is not yours for you to be praised on its account, nor is my ugliness mine for me to be blamed on its account. That is merely the work of the Fashioner; so whoever finds fault with the work finds fault with the Creator."

7

Aristotle said, "Everyone has a resemblance to an animal or something else. For example, one who takes by speed is like a wolf, one who takes by cunning is like a fox, and one who is simple-minded is like a donkey. One who has a good appearance without inner worth is like an oleander, one who is outwardly praiseworthy but inwardly blameworthy is like a date, and one who has a despised exterior but inward excellence is like an almond. And some combine all that is praiseworthy, like the citron, which combines pleasant appearance with nice fragrance and flavor."

Knowledge and Ignorance

1

Pythagoras said to a pupil of his who attached little importance to knowledge, "Young man, if you will not take pains for knowledge, you will suffer the distress of ignorance."

2

Seeing a handsome youth who was uneducated and uncultivated, Diogenes said, "However the house may be, it has no foundation."

3

Socrates said, "The polish of souls is geometry; the rust of souls is indulgence in animal lusts."

4

Aristotle said, "Leisure spent in idleness has sweet roots but bitter fruits; trouble taken in the pursuit of education has bitter roots but sweet fruits."

5

Plato said, "The knowledgable one knows the ignorant, having once also been ignorant; but the ignorant one does not know the knowledgable, never having been knowledgable."

6

Plato said, "Knowledge and fortune are of no benefit to one who gets them by theft, or to one who gets them by fraud, because these two depravities only take root in a deranged soul, in which nothing of its potential thrives or bears fruit."

7

Socrates was asked, "Why don't you record your wisdom in books?"

He replied, "How trusting you are of the skins of dead

animals, and how powerful your suspicion of living, eternal essences! You want to learn from a lode of ignorance, and you despair of learning from the source of intelligence!"

8

Plato said, "As long as you are able to add another's light to your own light, then do it."

9

Aristotle said, "Education graces the wealth of the wealthy, and veils the poverty of the poor."

Negativity

1

Pythagoras was asked, "What enervates a man and consumes him?"

The philosopher replied, "Anger and envy; but anxiety is worse than both!"

2

Aristotle was asked, "Why is it that the envious are always sorrowing?"

Aristotle replied, "Because they sorrow not only at any adversity that befalls them, they sorrow equally at any good that is granted to other people."

3

Socrates said, "Be wary of anger, for when it breaks out it distracts the angry one from everything, until he becomes like a house afire, which fills with shouting and smoke, to the point where no eye can see there, and no ear can hear."

He also said, "Just as one who is drunk cannot know the ugliness of drunkenness as long as he is drunk, until he sees it in another, similarly one who is angry cannot know the ugliness of anger except by seeing its influence on another."

Socrates also said, "Just as leanness of face, jaundice of the nostrils, and hollowness of the eyes are among the signs of death in sick bodies, similarly the change of the face through anger is a sign of death of the soul."

4

Aristotle said, "Cupidity is an individual's seeking what he doesn't have, while stinginess is his begrudging of what he has."

5

Plato was asked, "How does it happen that stupidity is more fortunate than intelligence?"

He replied, "Because evil infects intelligence, whereas evil does not infect stupidity, since it is itself evil, and evil does not infect an evil."

6

Aristotle said, "Specialties of evil include admonition of enemies and meanness to friends."

7

Pythagoras said, "Lack of cultivation is a cause of every evil."

8

Aristotle said, "A malicious person is an enemy to himself, so how can he be a friend to another?"

9

Plato said, "Evil people look for people's faults, ignoring their good qualities, just as flies look for rotten parts of a body, ignoring the wholesome."

10

Aristotle said, "An evil disposition is infectious."

He was asked, "How is that?"

He replied, "Because your companion does bad and does good, and when he does that a lot, you become similar to him."

11

Pythagoras said, "Three things make the earth quake: the slave who rules, the ignoramus who is sated, and the man whose wife is despised."

12

Plato said, "The unworthiness of a man is known by two things: he talks a lot about what is of no use to him, and he tells of what is not asked of him and not desired of him."

13

Aristotle said, "Affection and well-being are united against their enemies, anger and malice, which are harmful to them."

14

Socrates was asked, "What is the worst of states?"

He replied, "Decrepitude and destitution."

15

A man said to Aristotle that Plato was stupid. Aristotle said, "If someone else told you this, don't believe him; and if it is you who tell that, I don't believe you."

16

Plato said, "One who pays attention to a statement is a confederate of the speaker."

17

When a certain person was insolent to him, Aristotle said to him, "Graceful forgiveness is better, in our view, than requital for your offense. We have no recompense for your offense except forbearance, and no remedy for your outrage but patience.

"We have, in fact, already seen enough of your obvious inferiority to make us wish to be kind to you and forgiving to you. So do not presume to yourself that I would give up my good nature for your bad nature, or that I would pay you back by doing as you have done, or that I would go your way, for to requite evil with evil is to enter into it."

18

Plato said, "When the form of evil operates invisibly, it produces anxiety; and when it operates visibly, it produces suffering."

19

Pythagoras said, "When there is no firewood, fire goes out; and when no one is quarrelsome, argument ends."

20

Diogenes was asked, "Why are you called a cynic?"

He replied, "Because I confront people of evil and falsehood with truth, and I tell them the truth about themselves. And I fawn on the good and growl in the faces of the bad."

Realism

1

Pythagoras said, "If you want yourself, your family, your children, and your loved ones to live in security forever, then you are an ignoramus, wishing for yourself something you cannot have."

2

Pythagoras said, "If you want your son or your servant not to make mistakes, you are seeking something unnatural."

3

Pythagoras said, "When you call your son, your errand boy, or your servant, bear in mind the degree of obedience or insubordination of the one you are calling, and the fact that he may obey you or disobey you, in order that this too may inform your confidence and let you know about them, so that you do not make them a cause of trouble in your life."

4

Pythagoras said, "Just as faces are not alike, hearts are not alike."

Pleasure

1

Socrates said, "The greatest dominion is that man overcomes his passions."

2

Asked about pleasure, Pythagoras said, "Not everything that is pleasurable is beneficial, but everything that is beneficial is pleasurable."

3

Asked about sleep, Pythagoras said, "Sleep is a light death, and death is a long sleep."

4

Socrates said, "Pleasure is a honey snare."

5

A jester said to Socrates, "You have forbidden yourself the amenities of the world."

Socrates retorted, "And what are the amenities of the world?"

The jester said, "Fine meats and sweet wines, sumptuous clothing and beautiful women."

Socrates told him, "I give that to those who are content to be like swine and apes, and who are like beasts of prey in that their stomachs are graves of animals, and who prefer the structure of the unstable body to the structure of the eternal spirit."

Family and Friends

1

Pythagoras said, "A man should be good with his family at all times, so they will not be unable to be an adornment to him among his friends."

2

Pythagoras said, "Sitting on a roof's edge is better than living with a turbulent woman."

3

Pythagoras said, "A neighbor nearby is more helpful than a brother far away."

4

Socrates used to take shelter in a barrel with a little dog. Some of his students asked, "What are you doing with this dog?"

Socrates said, "The dog treats me better, since it protects me and doesn't annoy me, whereas you desert me and yet annoy me too!"

Mind and Matter

1

When a rich man expressed disapproval of Socrates, the philosopher said, "You would not be able to live as I live even if you wanted to, whereas I would be able to live as you do if I wanted to. And if you had known poverty, it would have kept you too occupied with yourself to feel sorry for Socrates!"

2

Socrates said, "Do not be bent on the acquisition of wealth at the expense of scattering your thoughts. Disregard death so that you do not die. Kill the passions, and you will be immortal. Adhere to justice, and safety will stay by you."

3

Socrates was asked, "Why do you never sorrow?"

He replied, "Because I never acquire anything whose loss would sadden me."

4

Aristotle was asked, "What things should an intelligent person acquire?"

He replied, "Those things which will swim with you when your ship sinks."

5

Plato said, "Don't let your holdings consist of things that will depart from you."

6

A philosopher wrote to Socrates, censuring him for eating little and wearing worn clothing, saying, "You maintain that compassion is incumbent upon all who are imbued with spirit and soul. You yourself are imbued with spirit and soul, yet you oppress them by paucity of nourishment and coarseness of clothing."

Socrates replied, "You have praised me to my face, which is actually disparagement. You have censured me for coarse clothing, but it has happened that a man will fall passionately in love with a homely woman and leave a comely one. And you have reproved me for eating little, but I only eat to live, whereas you live to eat. Peace!"

7

Socrates was asked, "Why don't you purchase some land?"

He replied, "Because I am ashamed before the Owner of the whole earth to dispute over a little patch of it, seeing as how the Owner is gracious and good to me!"

He was told, "But the Owner has granted it to you!"

Socrates responded, "Had it been *given* to me, I would not be made responsible for its produce."

He was told, "Then you could be as its manager, with you living in the middle of it."

Socrates retorted, "The pay is up to the Owner, but the manager may be faithless."

8

Aristotle had a valuable country estate, which he put in the care of a manager and did not personally superintend. Someone asked him why he did that; he said, "I did not acquire an estate by virtue of my commitment to properties, but by virtue of my commitment to my education; and by that means, I hope to acquire more properties."

9

Plato said, "He is not a consummate sage who rejoices at the wealth of the world, or sorrows at anything of its misfortunes."

10

When Socrates was imprisoned, and they assumed he was going to be executed, his students said to him, "Teacher, what do you instruct us to do with your body when you have been executed?"

Socrates replied, "The one who will worry about that is whoever needs the space, or whoever is vexed by the stench of my rotting corpse."

Friends and Enemies

1

Pythagoras said, "It is better to be struck by a true friend than to be kissed by an enemy."

2

Socrates said, "Among the things that show your friend's intelligence and his sincere advice to you as well as to himself is that he shows you your flaws and expels them from you; he exhorts you to what is best, and also accepts such exhortation from you; and he restrains you from evil, and is restrained from it by you."

3

Alexander said, "A man's enemies may sometimes be more beneficial to him than his friends, because they show him his faults, so he turns away from them, fearing their malice, thus keeping his good fortune, and he is on his guard against its loss as far as he is able."

4

Plato said, "Don't make friends with someone who is evil, for your character will take evil from his character without your being aware of it."

5

Socrates was asked, "What is the most beneficial thing a person can acquire?"

He answered, "A friend who gives sincere advice."

6

Aristotle said, "Whoever gives money to a friend has given of what he has accumulated, but one who gives a friend affection and sincere advice has given of himself."

7

Alexander said, "I have benefited more from my enemies than from my friends, because my enemies blame me for a mistake, calling my attention to it, whereas my friends present a mistake in a favorable light to me, encouraging me in it."

8

Socrates was asked, "Who is the most contemptible of people?"

He replied, "One who trusts no one and whom no one trusts."

9

Plato said, "It is a most serious matter for one to be mistaken about someone one trusts."

10

Alexander was asked, "How did you acquire such a mighty kingdom in spite of your youth?"

He said, "By winning over enemies and making them friends, and by obligating friends through beneficence to them."

11

Plato was asked, "How can one take revenge against one's enemy?"

He replied, "By becoming better oneself."

12

Plato also said, "When one of your peers envies you for an excellence that is apparent in you, and strives to inconvenience you or fabricates lies against you about things you have not said, do not counter him with the likes of his attack on you, for he will then excuse himself for his offense against you, and you will open a way for him to do what he wants to you. Instead, you should strive to increase that very excellence for which he envies you; for then you will hurt him without giving him a cause against you."

13

Plato said, "Your behavior with your friend should be conduct that does not make you need an arbitrator; and with enemies, conduct by which you will succeed in arbitration."

14

Plato said, "Do not befriend evil people, for the most they can give you is safety from them."

15

Socrates was asked, "Who is the worst of people?"
He replied, "One who helps you follow caprice."

16

Aristotle said, "One who annoys you with truth shows you good will, while one who pleases you with falsehood debases you."

17

Socrates said, "The error in giving to the undeserving is the same as withholding from the deserving."

Justice

1

Seeing his wife weeping as he was being taken out to be executed, Socrates said to her, "What makes you weep?"

She replied, "How could I not weep, when you are being killed unjustly?"

Socrates said, "What? Do you prefer that I be killed justly?"

2

It was related that two sophists, Batil the Useless and Fatin the Clever, passed by Socrates as he was being taken off to be executed. They, for their part, had gone to someone to arbitrate in a matter of dispute that they were contesting between them. Now they heard an on-looker exclaim, "He who sentenced you to death has done you wrong, Socrates!"

But Socrates said, "This man's words imply that he is gloating over my misfortune, or that he is commiserating with me, or that he has testimony for me, or that he is making a drunken jest."

The man was then questioned about what information he had, and he did in fact have testimony. Socrates declared, "Urgently as I may need to accept his testimony by pronouncement of his integrity and attestation of his honorable record, nevertheless it is not permissible to accept testimony for a judgment from someone upon whose head there lies deception."

As it turned out, the man who had the testimony was in the habit of dying his hair.

Now Fatin the Clever said to his companion, "If the arbitrator between us had been Socrates, who made this judicious distinction with knowledge of his imminent death, we would not have feared that he would err in his view or be unfair in his judgment."

3

Socrates said, "It is by justice that the universals of the world exist, and its particulars cannot exist without it."

4

It was related that once Socrates was at a reception where the servant was slow with the food. A man said to the host, "You should punish him as severely as you can."

But Socrates said, "No. Forgive him his mistake; for to improve yourself at the cost of spoiling your servant is better than correcting your servant at the cost of corrupting yourself."

Self-Government

1

Socrates said, "It is desirable that thought should rule before an act, during the act, and after the act: before the act, so that it will not be mean and hurtful; during the act, so that it does not cause a nuisance; and after the act, so that it may be followed up and it may be known what it has led to, and its beginning may be assessed by its end."

2

Socrates said, "Kill desire, and you enliven nature."

3

Socrates said, "Treat anger with silence, and desire with anger; for whoever is angered at himself because of experiencing its disadvantages is diverted from it."

4

Socrates said, "Don't be afraid of death, for the bitterness of it lies in the fear of it."

5

An ignorant young man asked Plato, "How did you manage to learn so much?"

Plato said, "It is because I have burned more oil than you have drunk wine."

6

Someone said, in the presence of Socrates, "Silence is safer, because mistakes happen when one talks a lot."

Socrates remarked, "That doesn't happen to someone who knows what he's talking about. In the case of someone who does not know what he's talking about, though, he'll make mistakes whether he talks a little or a lot."

7

Socrates was asked, "Who does one ask for advice in one's affairs?"

He replied, "The man who is human in deed and not merely in form; for he is above the time. One who is under the time does not see the consequence of anything in it, so he is not consulted in coming to a decision about something."

8

When Aesop was taken captive, a man who wanted to buy him said, "Shall I buy you?"

Aesop said, "How can you buy me to be your slave after you have taken me as an adviser?"

9

Socrates said, "Your days are three. There is the day that has gone by, which you cannot overtake. Then there is the day you are in, of which you ought to avail yourself. As for your tomorrow, all you can do is hope. But do not rely on hope so much that you neglect work.

"Today and tomorrow are in the position of two brothers. One of them stopped over at your house, but you treated him badly and unhospitably, so he left, blaming you. Then his brother came to you after that and said, 'Hey you! I came to you after my brother, who left you yesterday, and whom you mistreated by your actions. Now be good to me, and that will efface your mistreatment of him. Yet nothing could be more natural for you, if you inflict evil on me, that you be ruined by the testimony of both of us against you."

10

Pythagoras was asked, "What is hardest for a human being?"

He replied, "Knowing oneself and concealing inner thoughts."

11

Solon the philosopher was asked, "What is most difficult for a human being?"

He said, "To know one's own imperfections and refrain from what one should not speak of."

12

Pythagoras said, "There is no taking back something you have already said or done, so be wary before that."

13

Plato said, "We ought to turn away from base things. Base things are the world, so we ought to turn away from the world. And to turn away from the world is to be guided by God Most High."

14

When a man complained to him about his circumstances, Plato said, "You will find people to be one of two kinds: there is the one who suffers setback on his own account but his luck has advanced him, and there is the one who has progressed on his own account but his time has set him back. So either be content by choice with your circumstances, or you will have to be content by force of circumstances."

15

Socrates said, "When your self asks you for provision for tomorrow, say, 'Get me a guarantee for today!'"

16

Plato said, "It is no wonder when one in whom passions have died out becomes virtuous; the wonder is when one whose passions contend with him is at the same time virtuous."

17

Plato was asked, "Why, of all the cities of Greece, did you choose the city of Academy Garden, seeing as how it is a pestilent place?"

He replied, "So that if I do not refrain from passions for fear of harm to the soul, I will refrain from them out of necessity, to avoid the invasion of harm into the body."

18

Plato said, "Place intelligence on your right and truth on your left, and you will be safe all your life and remain free."

Priorities

1

When Socrates was told that the speech he gave at a certain time was not accepted, he retorted, "I am not worried about whether it is accepted; I am worried about whether I spoke well on that occasion."

2

Plato said, "One who raises himself above lowly ambitions becomes known for his good qualities. One who is known for his good qualities is praised, and one who is praised is loved. But humanity loves no one until God has loved that one."

3

Socrates saw a young man who had inherited money from his father but had squandered it, to the point where he was reduced to eating olives and bread. Socrates said, "Young man, if you had restricted yourself to food like this, this would not be your food."

The Life of the World

1

Socrates said, "Life has two boundaries: one goes as far as work, the other goes as far as the instant of death. The first one maintains it, the second terminates it."

2

Socrates said, "The world is desired for three things: power, wealth, and comfort. But one who is abstemious in the world grows strong, one who is content grows rich, and one with little ambition is at ease."

3

Anaxarsis said, "The grapevine bears three bunches of grapes: first, a bunch of enjoyment; second, a bunch of intoxication; and third, a bunch of folly."

4

Aristotle said, "Don't crave the world, for you only stay in it a little while; how long can you possibly live?"

5

Plato said, "When the transcendent Creator only wishes for the world what is good for it, our joy and our sorrow are useless."

Spiritual Perception

1

A man said to Plato, "You are the one who says there is a world other than this one, and a human being other than this one."

Plato said, "Yes."

The man said, "Then show me."

Plato said, "You don't have what it takes to see it."

2

Pythagoras was asked, "Why did you come to this world?"

The philosopher replied, "It was not my idea, not my preference! But I saw, where I was, a beautiful picture, and I said, 'Let me have this.' But I was told, 'Not until you journey to this country to carry out an intelligence mission for us, give an account of a wonder, and establish a way of access to us. We will furnish you with provisions, and do our best to help you.'

"So I crossed valleys and peaks, dangers and perils, until I reached this place. And here I am, as I was instructed in the beginning.

"But I see I have enemies here of whom I had no knowledge there, and I have made my way alternately socializing with them and fighting them, until I have come to the point where I am unable to do it anymore. So I fear I may be overcome, and denied everything I was promised."

He was asked, "Why didn't you stay where you were?"

Pythagoras said, "Folks, don't blame me! If you had witnessed what I witnessed, you would have demanded it more, even if the terror were greater and the menace were worse. For whoever profit delights, crossing land and sea is easy!"

3

Aristotle said, "There is Something above the substance of the firmament; nothing is greater than It, and there is no way to quantify or measure It. It is beyond change in any manner or mode. There is no limit to Its power. Therefore It performs Its acts outside of time, being by nature effective and thus always in action, without Its action affecting It. Nothing comes from It in a state of potential; rather, things come from It in action, while Its potential always pervades the universe."

4

Aristotle said, "By the arrangement of things, their connectedness, their concord, and their order, we know that their Maker is one."

5

Someone asked Socrates, "What is God the Exalted like?"

Socrates answered, "Hidden, but not concealed; evident, but not visible."

6

Hermes said, "It is indeed difficult to know or talk about the reality of the Creator, for it is not possible for a graspable body to describe what is ungraspable, and what is not perfect does not comprehend what is perfect, and it is hard to connect the eternal with what is not eternal, for the eternal abides forever, while what is not eternal passes away. And that which passes away is imagination, shadow; and the relationship between that which passes away and God, who does not die, is as that between the weak and the strong, or the lowly and the noble."

Political Science

1

Plato said, "When a nation is tolerant of malpractice in judges and doctors, it is then decadent and near to disintegration."

2

Plato said, "It behooves a ruler to start by rectifying himself before he starts rectifying his citizenry, lest he be in the situation of one who wants to straighten a crooked shadow before straightening the rod of which it is the shadow."

3

Plato said, "A state starts out with a crude model, then applies realities and perfects obedience to God and to those in authority.

"Then when it has gotten rid of its enemies and its people are secure, their defense against their enemies begins to deprive them of the chance to get some of the bounty available to them.

"Then when they become immersed in the abundance and luxury of life they enjoy, they are too preoccupied with recreation to be of any help. This reaches the point where their social order cannot withstand anyone who has designs on them, and the regime comes to an end.

"They are like fruits, which at first are too unripe to eat, then you see them in an intermediate condition, and then they mature; yet along with their delicious sweetness, the fruits are closest to rotting and changing."

4

Plato said, "States begin with justice and fear. Then when they reach midway in development, they are governed by ambition and fear. And when their passing is near, they are governed by ambition and favoritism."

5

Pythagoras said, "Prefer being defeated but just to being victorious but unjust."

6

Plato said, "The decline of a state includes cleaving to secondary things and neglecting basics, abandonment of works, neglect of construction, extension of hostilities, and infringement of agreements."

7

Plato said, "The most beloved of people to a ruler is one whose weakness he reckons to be completely in his passions, and his strength to be entirely in his opinion and his conservatism."

8

Plato said, "The first exercise of a prime minister is tolerance of the morals of the masses and concealment of ire; and attention to the morals of the ruler in his relations with others. If the ruler is harsh and rude, the minister deals with people otherwise; and if the ruler is mild and easygoing, the minister deals with people more firmly, in order to approach justice in his work."

9

Plato said, "A king is not the one who rules over slaves and *hoi polloi*, but the one who governs the free and the advantaged. And the wealthy one is not the one who amasses money, but the one who manages it well and knows how to save and to spend."

10

Plato said, "Among the characteristics of a free man is that his patience in the betterment of those below him is greater than his patience in seeking the favor of those above him, and he tolerates more from those who are weaker than he tolerates from those who are stronger."

11

Plato said, "Clemency is attributable only to one who has the power to attack."

12

Aristotle said, "When the ruler is just, the judge is honest, and the chief of police is a good manager, the reign lasts and its normal way of life is well established and does not fall into oblivion; otherwise, they become vitiated and pass away."

13

Plato said, "The time of a tyrannical ruler is shorter than the time of a just one, because the tyrant is a spoiler and the just one is a restorer; and spoiling something is quicker than restoring it."

Speech and Silence

1

Plato said, "The difference between silence and inability to express oneself is that silence is keeping the tongue from speaking even while knowing what to say, whereas inability to express oneself is keeping the tongue from speaking because of not knowing what to say."

2

Plato said, "When you talk to someone who knows more than you do, get right to the point, without unnatural wordiness and without embellishment. But when you talk to someone who knows less than you do, expand your speech so that he may get in the end what he could not at first."

3

Plato said, "Expansiveness is one thing that makes you partially blind, so do not be free with it except to someone who is trustworthy in respect to it and is deserving of it."

4

A philosopher wrote to Socrates, saying, "I know the reason you eat so little; but why do you speak so little? You are stingy to yourself with food, and stingy to others with words!"

Socrates replied, "What I need to leave alone, and what I need to leave to others, are no business of yours; and to bother with what is none of your business is too much trouble!

"As for the paucity of my words, I see that God the Blessed and Exalted has made for me two ears and one mouth, so I may listen twice as much as I speak. You, on the other hand, talk more than you listen, and one who talks too much is accused of nonsense and fabrication, of babbling and lying."

5

Aristotle said, "When you want to know if a man is master of his desires, then observe how much control he has over what he says."

6

Asked about rhetoric, Aristotle described it as, "Putting much meaning in few words, and putting a little meaning in many words."

7

Asked what is most difficult, Aristotle said, "Silence."

Education

1

Aristotle was asked, "What is the best of animals?"
He replied, "The human being graced with education."

2

Isocrates said, "It behooves a cultured person to take the best part of all aspects of education, just as the bee takes the best part of every flower."

3

Aristotle said, "Education is an adornment for the rich, and a way of life for the poor, by which they live the life of the free."

4

Aristotle was asked, "What graces a man among his fellows?"

He replied, "Education graces the wealth of the wealthy and conceals the poverty of the poor."

5

Plato said, "When you admonish a wrongdoer, do so gently, that it may not lead to open hostility."

6

Socrates was asked, "What is most gratifying in the world?"

He said, "Culture, education, and seeing what one has not seen before."

7

Aristotle said, "Habituate the self to the humanities, for from them and in them are seen the wonders of thought and the subtleties of reflection."

8

Aristotle said, "When the intelligence is sound, education adheres to it as nutrients are incorporated into a healthy body, nurturing it and making it grow. When the intelligence is impaired, it withdraws from any education it is taught, just as someone suffering from a stomach ailment cannot hold down the food he eats. And when an ignoramus chooses to learn something, that education transforms within him into folly, just as wholesome food in the stomach of a sick man turns into disease."

Part Two

Sayings of Plato

Truth

Plato said to his companions, "When you attain truth, it blesses you, and when you abandon truth, it curses me. So make truth your own and act on it, and be wary of error; for therein lies God's satisfaction with you, and my affection for you."

He also said, "Truth is removal of the veil."

Pride

The best of what is in pride is being too proud to indulge in the vices of the people, and shunning servility to excess.

Attention

Don't slight a small matter from which a serious matter may arise.

Arrogance

Don't be arrogant in victory.

Compassion

Don't laugh at another's mistake.

Don't rejoice at another's fall.

Anger

Don't argue with someone who is angry.

Put up with mistakes from people in a reasonable way.

Gluttony

Refrain from making your insides coffins and graves of animals.

Antagonism

Let your dread of your strategy against your enemy be greater than your dread of your enemy's strategy against you.

Noble and Ignoble

The noble one rises with all who know him, while the ignoble one rises by himself.

Humility

Do not look down on anyone because of his humility; rather, honor him more for his humility.

When an intelligent person is commended for a virtue he does not have, it is not proper that he accept that commendation.

Charity

One who hesitates over a charitable deed should not disdain the work involved.

Conscience

You should do what is essential without anyone impelling you to do it, and refrain from uncalled-for action without a prohibition forbidding you from doing it.

Goodness
When the form of good operates invisibly, it produces happiness; and when it operates visibly, it produces delight.

Disposition
There are some people whose disposition is suited for something beyond which they cannot go.

Work
One who chooses to be happy is a lover of labor.

Desire and Intellect
When times change for the better, desires serve intellects; and when times change for the worse, intellects serve desires.

Fortune
Fortune never gives anyone anything without taking it away.

Tact and Truthfulness
When you are with an intelligent man, please him even to the annoyance of those around him; but when you are with a man of weak perception, go ahead and annoy him, even to the pleasure of his subordinates.

Forgiveness

Forgiveness corrupts mean people to the same degree that it improves noble people.

Virtues

Most virtues are disagreeable at first but end up sweet.

Chivalry

The purpose of chivalry is for a man to have a sense of shame on his own account. And that is because the reason for a sense of shame before an elder is not his age or the whiteness of his beard; the reason for a sense of shame before him is the illumination of the essence of the intelligence in him. So when that radiant essence is in us, we ought to have a sense of shame before it, and not approach it shamelessly.

Prosperity and Affliction

The insolence of a man in prosperity corresponds to his humility in affliction.

Progress

Do not antagonize a progressive nation, lest you turn back its progress.

Stinginess

The souls of stingy people are more strongly shackled than the souls of generous people.

Part Three

Sayings of Aristotle

Definitions

Definitions are of four kinds: transcendental, descriptive, logical, and physical.

The transcendental deals with categories of things that are not material forms and are not connected to material forms, and with the elucidation of their differences.

As for the descriptive, that is the definition of things whose substances cannot be distinguished except in imagination.

The logical is the sort employed by dialectitians, who define things in relation to their purpose and form.

As for the physical definition, that deals with categories of things in relation to both their matter and form together.

Intellect

Aristotle said, "Everything has a skill, and the skill of the intellect is choosing well."

He also said, "Intelligence is a means to a profitable life."

Unreality and Untruth

The unreal is what does not exist at all; the untrue is what is either exaggerated or understated.

Humankind

Humankind is elevated above all animals only by speech and intellect; so if one is mute and uncomprehending, one reverts to animality.

Logic

Logic is a tool for all sciences.

Philosophy

Asked how many things are required for a person to become a philosopher, Aristotle said, "Three things: need, disposition, and interest."

Value

There is nothing in the universe without value, for nature does nothing in vain.

Generosity

The generous one is the one who neither withholds generosity nor mixes it with extravagance.

Frugality

When a rich man eats a meager meal of humble food, it is said he only did it to heal himself thereby, but when a poor man eats it, it is said that neediness drove him to it.

Compulsion and Choice

A human being is under compulsion in the form of having choice.

Consumption and Absorption
Increase in strength is due not to the quantity of nutrients with which you supply your body, but to the quantity of what it absorbs.

Four Ears
Have four ears: one pair to listen to what is important to you, and one pair for what does not concern you, so that what is of concern and what is not should not be brought together in one.

Intelligence and Decency
Decency is not cheating anyone, and intelligence is not being cheated by anyone.

Culture and Society
To be in combat without arms is easier than to enter a gathering without understanding.

Revelation and Concealment
Asked what should be revealed and what should be concealed, Aristotle said, "You show gratitude for a benefactor, and you conceal the imperfection of anyone you raise to the status of a true friend."

Enrichment
Asked how a man becomes wealthy, Aristotle replied, "In the case of a ruler, through service; in the case of the general run of humanity, through reliability and efficiency."

Patience
Aristotle said, "Whoever does not have intelligent patience has neither the world nor the hereafter."

When Aristotle went to Alexander to express sympathy on account of a misfortune that had befallen him, he said, "I did not come to you to offer condolence for your trouble, but to learn patience, for I know that you know patience in misfortune is a virtue. Your character, furthermore, is purged of all depravity; and how could you be induced to be the way you naturally are, or taught to behave as you normally do?"

Cultural Gifts
Aristotle wrote to Alexander, "God distributed gifts among peoples, giving bravery to the Persians, horsemanship to the Eastern Tribes, artistry to the Byzantines, and subtlety and philosophy to the Indians."

Righteousness
Among the signs of a righteous man are that he is friendly to his friends' friends and hostile to their enemies.

Friendship
Aristotle said, "Trust in and count on a friend who is knowledgable; and don't be too fearful, like a slave or a weakling. Do not trust in a friend who is ignorant and greedy, and beware of an enemy who is dissolute and ignorant."

He also said, "One who has no friends has no family and no home; and one who has no family and children has no name and no posterity."

Life and Death

One who is perpetually needy, or chronically ill, or seized with fear, or away from his family and children for a long time, or who makes a living by begging from others, should consider his life as death and his death as repose.

Passion and Intelligence

When passion overcomes intelligence, it changes the good qualities that are the beauty of intelligence into bad qualities, turning patience into resentment, knowledge into hypocrisy, intelligence into craftiness, culture into conceit, eloquence into prattle, liberality into wastefulness, frugality into stinginess, and forgiveness into cowardice.

When this happens to someone, it leaves one so that one sees no health but physical health, no knowledge but that by which one becomes presumptuous, no wealth but monetary profit, no confidence but in material acquisition, and no security but in subjugation of people.

All of that is inconsistent with one's aim, distancing one from one's object and bringing one nearer to perdition.

But when intelligence overcomes passion, it changes the bad qualities into good ones, turning stupidity into discernment, vehemence into acumen, cunning into intelligence, prattle into eloquence, inarticulateness into silence, unruliness into cultivation, recklessness into energy, cowardice into caution, prodigality into liberality, and stinginess into frugality.

The Happy Man
The happy man is the intelligent one whose intelligence is his most perfect characteristic and whose knowledge is his most excellent provision, who is only enriched by contentment, who is only made secure by innocence, who is compelled by increase only to gratitude, and who is shielded from adversities only by prayer.

But one who is void of intelligence is not made more powerful by formal authority, and one who has no contentment is not made richer by material wealth.

Three Falsehoods
A ruler who lies does not count as a ruler, a pious ascetic who deceives does not count as a pious ascetic, a friend who leaves you in a lurch does not count as a friend, and one who does a favor for an ingrate does not count as a benefactor.

Despondency
An intelligent person should not be despondent, for two reasons: either he has a way to get rid of the misfortune that has happened to him, and so he works on it on his own, with a heart undistracted by sorrow; or if he does not see any way to deal with what has happened to him

or any way to get rid of it, then he directs himself to a means of being patient.

Charity
A charitable person is not one who seeks to do good only to the good and not the bad, but one who embraces both of them with good. Have you not seen the veracious person speaking truth to someone who has lied to him, and the trustworthy person discharging a trust for someone who has let him down, and the just person being just to one who has oppressed him? Thus is the charitable person good to one who has been bad to him, and forgiving to one who has wronged him, and generous to one who has been stingy to him.

Troubles
Troubles turn an enemy into a friend, if he is noble; they turn an envious person into a compassionate one, if he is intelligent; they turn a commoner into a prince, if he is patient.

Sincerity
The sincerest friend, in terms of affection, is one whose affection does not come from desire or fear.

Conductors to Truth
We should be grateful to the forbears of a people who were our initiators into contact with something of truth; so how about those who became our actual way to truth!

Obligation

Just as you prefer others being in your debt to your being in their debt, so should your doing good for others be preferable to you over their doing good for you.

Caution, Astuteness, and Mindfulness

Be cautious, as though you were inexperienced; be astute, as though you were negligent; be mindful, as though you were forgetful.

Condolences

Aristotle wrote to a noble lady of his family to console her on the loss of a brother of hers: "I dislike to rush you with encouragement to bear up at the beginning of the calamity, because it is hard for one giving consolation to resist the rush of sadness, just as it is hard for a swimmer to face the current. But it is not graceful for one like you, who are a descendant of people remembered for bravery and greatness of resolve, to show immoderation in grieving, particularly in the case of an event such as has touched you.

"For he parted from this world praised and remembered for the magnanimity of his acts and the greatness of his virtues; and then his death was the best of deaths. Anyone who betrayed him or broke a compact with him will be haunted by censure and shame.

"Be aware that the eyes of the people are looking at you, watching how you will be in this situation. Show, therefore, greatness of will and patience in affliction, as befits your noble origins. Peace."

Seeking and Finding
A man said to Aristotle, "I have been in quest of knowledge for forty years."

Aristotle said, "Many a man who has engaged in commerce for forty years does not have goods for the day."

Leadership Qualities
When a man deals with someone who hates him such that he turns into one of his friends, and treats his friend with justice so that he does not go over to his enemies, he is worthy to be called a leader and to take responsibility for the conditions of governing.

Appropriate Feelings
One should become accustomed from youth to be happy about what one should be happy about, and to be sad about what one should be sad about.

Ponderous People
Aristotle was asked, "Why does a ponderous person weigh heavier on the heart than a heavy burden on the back?"

Aristotle replied, "Because the spirit helps the body with the heavy load, but the spirit bears the ponderous person alone."

Straight and Crooked

An intelligent individual harmonizes with another intelligent one, but an ignoramus harmonizes with neither an intelligent person nor another ignoramus. That is like something straight fitting something straight, whereas something crooked fits neither something crooked nor something straight.

Seek the Eternal

Do not take a liking to what passes away and whose end is near. Seek the wealth that does not perish, and the life that does not change, the kingdom that never ends, and the permanence that does not dwindle away.

Self-Improvement

Improve yourself for your own sake, and people will follow you.

Here and Hereafter

Make your life in this world a defense for your afterlife; do not make your afterlife a defense for your life in this world.

Part Four

Meditations of the Greek Master

1

The Primary Agent is still, without any sort of movement at all. Its stillness produces its image, which is the intellect; but not in a thing, for its image is a vessel, noble and powerful, superior in nobility and power to all lower vessels.

In that image are all science and knowledge, because when it emanated from the Primary Agent, it focused on its cause, and beheld it according to its power and thus became intellect and essence.

This essence is the intellect. So it was primary in its relation to what is subordinate to it, and secondary in relation to what is above it.

2

Whoever wishes to know how the true One creates a multiplicity of phenomena should set his gaze on the true One alone, leaving aside all things, which come from It; and should return to Its essence and stay there: for he will see, by means of his intellect, the true One, motionless, standing high above all things intelligible and sensible.

And he will see the totality of things as if they were productions emanated from It and inclining to It. In this way, things start to move, meaning that it is necessary for everything in motion to have something toward which to move, and there is nothing in motion but what moves attracted to what it comes from, for it only desires to attain to It and to assimilate to It.

3

The Primary Agent is necessarily still, without movement, insofar as there must be something secondary to It. And Its action must be something secondary to It. And Its action must be without deliberation, movement, or desire inclining to the effect.

The primary effect is the intellect, which emanated from the potency and power of the stillness of the Agent. Then the totality of intelligible and sensible phenomena emanated from It by the mediation of the intellect.

4

The intellect became all things only because its Creator is not like anything whatsoever. And the primary Creator does not resemble anything whatsoever because all things come from It, and because It has no attributes and no particular form inherent in it.

And that is because the primary Creator is one, its oneness meaning that it is unconditioned. It has no properties of Its own, because all properties emanate from It. Thus all things are in It, while it is not in any thing, except as cause.

5

All things are in the intellect, and it is in things. Things happen to be in the intellect because their forms are in it, and have emanated from it into things, since it is the cause of things lower than it.

However, although the intellect is the cause of things below it, nevertheless it is not the whole cause of a thing, being only the cause of the form of the thing, not the cause of its essence.

As for the Primary Agent, It is the overall cause, because It is the unmediated cause of the essence of the thing, and the cause of the essence of the soul and the forms of things, through the mediation of the intellect.

And the soul and all things are formed in the intellect. They are not in the Primary Cause; they are only emanated from It.

6

All intelligible phenomena are delimited. The limitation of a thing is the totality of its attributes and its form. That is because when the Primary Cause created the essence of things, It did not leave them dependent on something without definition, but on what delimits and encompasses, defining them by their forms.

For the boundary of a created thing is its form and stability. And stability is characteristic of the intellect, defining it by the totality of its attributes. Stability is the normal state and constancy of the intellect and intelligible phenomena.

7

The unadulterated One is like light, while the secondary unit, which is related to something else, is like the sun; and the tertiary phenomenon is like the moon, which gets its light from the sun.

In the intellect is an essential luminosity, which, however, is not simply luminosity, but a substance that is a receptor of light. As for the thing that illumines the intellect and pours light upon it, that is simply light and nothing else but light. But it is an unrestricted light, pure and unadulterated, which pours its power on the intellect, making it an illuminating, enlightening intelligence.

However, the light that is in the intellect is a thing within a thing, whereas the light that illumines the intellect is not in something else. It is light alone, abiding steadily through its essence and illuminating all things. Some things, however, receive more of its light, and some receive less.

8

The true One is the creator of things, but It is not remote from them or separate from them. It is with all things, but is with them as if It were not with them. Its togetherness is evident only with those things that have the power to receive It.

9

The One is great, greater than all things; not in terms of mass, but in terms of power. Thus when we say It is infinite, we do not mean It is infinite in terms of mass or number, but that nothing encompasses Its power. And that is because it is above all possible imagination, permanently existing by virtue of Its own essence, void of attributes.

10

The One is good, not to Its own essence, for Its essence is goodness pure and true; rather, It is good to all things that have the power to receive the good It pours on them.

Furthermore, It has no motion, because it is before motion, before thought, and before knowledge. And there is nothing in It that it wants to know in the way a mortal knows. Rather, It is the knowledge that does not need to know by another knowledge, because It is pure ultimate knowledge, comprehending all knowledge as well as the cause of the sciences.

11

The first created intellect itself has no form. In relation to the primary Creator, it does have form, because it reaches a limit, whereupon it is defined and so comes to have attributes and form.

As for the primary Creator, It has no form, because there is no other thing above It that It would aim to reach, and nothing below It can reach It. So It is unlimited in every way, and thus happens to have no description and no form.

12

If the primary Creator were a form, the intellect would be a logos. But the intellect is not a logos, and there is no logos in it, for it was devised as a creation without its Creator having any attributes or form such that It could put that complex of attributes in there as a logos.

So the intellect is not a logos, nor is there a logos in it. But it is the fashioner of the logos in things, because it has attributes and characteristics. When it makes a thing, it imprints some of its attributes on the thing; and that imprint is the effective logos in the thing.

13

The primary One cannot be multiple in any way; otherwise the multiplicity that is in It would be attached to another, prior One. Rather, It must be one unadulterated Good. And It must be the Creator of a thing that is one, is good, and has the form of goodness, either as an imprint from the primary Creator, or as the imprint of Its imprint.

The imprint of the Creator is the intellect, and the imprint of the intellect is life. And life is also intellect, just as the imprint of fire is also fire.

However, it is not necessary that what is in the imprint is what is in that which makes the imprint, or what is not in it. That is because the primary imprinter is one, whereas its imprint is the intellect, and the intellect is two, because it is created, and the created as after the creator.

The imprint of the intellect is the soul, and in the intellect is what is in the soul, but there is in the soul what is not in the intellect. That is because the soul is more than two. For that reason, the soul comes to have predilections and act independently. Its independent action is its thought.

Each individual form continues to leave an imprint—and the imprints are more numerous than the form—until it comes to an imprint that does not itself leave an imprint on anything. So the first original imprints but is not imprinted, and the last thing is an imprint that does not make an imprint. And whatever is between the imprinter and the imprinted imprints what is below it and is imprinted by what is above it.

However, the first imprint, which is the intellect, operates an intellectual operation characterized by regularity without any deviation whatsoever, because it is an imprint from an absolutely motionless imprinter.

The second imprint, though, which is the soul, operates a psychological operation that is somewhat predisposed, since it is derived from an imprinter that is in motion. So the soul becomes the thinker.

Now the third imprint is the primal celestial noble body, which operates a local operation that is regular within the particular locale. It is only a local operation because it is an imprint from an operation that has a predisposed inclination, even though it is not itself a local operation.

The fourth imprint is the earthly bodies, which operate locally and erratically in both place and manner. So they become mutually opposed in positioning and in power.

All the imprints are connected to the initial action, which is the intellect; and the intellect is connected to the Primary Agent, which is the Creator and Preserver of them all, exept that It creates some of them without mediation, and some of them through mediation.

14

The Pure Good is the first to pour good upon things and clothe them in good, as the sun clothes physical objects with light, by which they shine.

15

The Primary Good is good, pure and simple, not by virtue of connection with something else, because there is nothing else above It. All things are below It, and receive good from It. It is, furthermore, an agent, though Its action is intellect, life, and self, and everything in which there is life and intelligence.

16

The further removed a thing is from matter, the greater the good in it. Whatever is close to matter and comes within its domain, the good in it lessens.

17

Evil is simply what is outstanding in the last things, which have not received anything from the Primary Good at all. And just as there is nothing else above the Primary Good, so there is nothing else below the evil things.

It should not be supposed that evil is opposite to the Primary Good, because there is no intermediary between them. The Primary Good, therefore, is that which has no opposite. Good either does not exist, or if it does exist, it has no opposite whatsoever. But it is impossible for Good not to exist, because it is the cause of things.

18

Asked what he had gotten from his love of knowledge, the Greek Master said, "When I am sorrowful, it is my consolation. When I am having a good time, it is my delight. When I am listless, it is my motivation. When I am energetic, it is my implement. When I am gloomy, it is my light. And when my gloom vanishes, it is my recreation and my pleasure."

19

The soul comes from that world to this one, and again from this world to that world.

20

Instruction is but reminder; the soul does not remember its state before its descent into the human body; but it does remember its states after its departure from the human body. If it is ignorant and infatuated with the physical nature, it yearns for its former surroundings and grieves intensely. But if it knows the vanity of this world, it rejoices in departure from the body and disdains this world so intensely that it flees to its own world.

Then when it has come to its own world, it remembers something of its former surroundings in this world. It comes to a state where it does not like this world to occur to its mind, because of the vileness and baseness of this world. And it looks upon powers and ideas, which fill it with enthusiasm, joy, and love for contemplation of all forms of knowledge, such that it is as if forgetful of everything of its surroundings in this world.

21

In the other world there is no memory, because there is no past and no future there. Rather, all existents and their forms are there at once. Everything the soul did in this world, and everything else with which it was concerned, is as if something present in its essence, by witness and not by memory.

Furthermore, when the soul departs from the physical world, it is united with the intellect, to be purified of the body and the senses, so that the soul and the intellect are as if one thing. Then the forms of all existents are present to it; so there is neither memory nor forgetfulness, but one single knowledge, complete and permanent.

22

The soul does not abide endlessly in this world. If this physical world were endless, the soul would remain in it endlessly. However, since the physical world is finite, it is not possible for the soul to abide in it for an endless time, because it makes the journey from the horizon to the center within a finite time.

23

In the natures of the things in this world are congruencies and differences, resulting in attraction and repulsion. Real magic is nothing but knowledge of these things within one another.

24

When we depart from this earthly world and go to that sublime world and unite with the universal soul, it is not hidden from us who we are, where we came from, where we went, and where we were.

25

When a human being is immersed in the desires of the natural body, he does not ascend rapidly. But if one is unattached to these things, and has taken to the intellect, then natural disposition cannot entice one.

26

All things are from the Creator, through the generosity thereof; and the first creation therefore is the primordial matter, then the intellect, then the soul, then the nature, then the body.

27

The Primal Good is the Creator, Exalted; and everything else is less good than It, to the extent of the intermediaries between them, because whatever is closer to the Exalted Creator has more goodness.

28

The Primal Good is that which does not cease to exist. The secondary good is what this Primary Good created, which is the intellect. Then the tertiary good is the soul, with its arrangement winding up in the bodies. So the good in the body is the soul, for without the soul its constituent parts would dissolve and it would not be a body.

29

All good comes to things from the Exalted Creator, by emanation and imprinting. So they have no power from primordial matter to preserve the health that is always beneficial to them. Rather, they have to renew it in one condition after another.

Part Five

Notes

The following notes from other wisdom traditions are taken from the following sources (all translations mine):

Taoist Huainan Masters: *The Book of Leadership and Strategy: Lessons of the Chinese Masters* (Boston: Shambhala, 1992).

Lao-tzu: *Sex, Health, and Long Life* (Boston: Shambhala, 1994).

Confucius: *The Essential Confucius* (San Francisco: HarperCollins, 1992).

I Ching: *The Essential Confucius* and *The Human Element: A Course in Resourceful Thinking* (Boston: Shambhala, 1994).

Wen-tzu: Wen-tzu: *Understanding the Mysteries* (Boston: Shambhala, 1992).

The Master of Demon Valley and the Master of the Hidden Storehouse: *Thunder in the Sky: Secrets on the Acquisition and Exercise of Power* (Boston: Shambhala, 1993).

Taoist master Liu I-ming: *Awakening to the Tao* (Boston: Shambhala, 1988).

Various Zen masters: *Zen Lessons: The Art of Leadership* (Boston: Shambhala, 1989).

Huanchu Daoren: *Back to Beginnings: Reflections on the Tao* (Boston: Shambhala, 1990).

Qur'an: *The Essential Koran* (San Francisco, HarperCollins, 1993).

Muhammad the Prophet: *The Wisdom of the Prophet: Sayings of Muhammad* (Boston: Shambhala, 1994).

Sufi master 'Ali: *Living and Dying with Grace: Counsels of Hadrat 'Ali* (Boston: Shambhala, 1995).

Money

1. Muhammad the Prophet said, "My heirs will not divide up a single coin. Whatever I leave, besides support for my wives and provision for my workers, is charity."

2. Muhammad the Prophet said, "A time is coming to humankind when the individual does not care whether his gains are ethical or ill-gotten."

3. Muhammad the Prophet said, "I dreamed that two men came to me and took me to a holy land, where we went on until we came to a river of blood. In it stood a man. By the river side there was another man, with stones in his hands, facing the man in the river. When the man tried to come out of the river, the other man threw a stone into his mouth and made him go back to where he had been. And he proceeded to throw a stone into the man's mouth each and every time he tried to come out, making him return to the state he had been in. I then asked, 'What is this?'" Then the Prophet explained, "The one I saw in the river was a profiteer."

4. 'Ali said, "The least of your duties to God is that you do not use God's blessings to help you do wrong."

   Muhammad the Prophet said, "If I had a mountain of gold, it would not please me if I still had any of it after three days, except something set aside for debts."

5. Muhammad the Prophet said, "God Most High has said, 'Spend, O child of Adam, and I will spend on you.'"

6. Muhammad the Prophet said, "Every single day the slaves of God pass, two angels come down. One says, 'O God, give every generous one recompense!' The other says, 'O God, give every miser ruination!'"

   'Ali said, "I am the leader of the faithful, while money is the leader of profligates."

7. Muhammad the Prophet said, "No one should envy anyone but two people: someone to whom God has given wealth and who is thus empowered to spend it righteously; and someone to whom God has given wisdom and who judges by it and teaches it."

8. Whenever food was brought to the Prophet Muhammad, he would ask if it was a gift, or alms for charity. If he was told it was alms for charity, the Prophet would tell his companions to eat it, and would not partake of it himself. If he was told it was a gift, he would eat with them.

9. Muhammad the Prophet said, "If someone is given wealth by God but does not pay the welfare tax, on the Day of Resurrection his wealth will be represented to him as a viper encircling him, striking him with two streams of poison. It will seize him by the jaws and say, 'I am your wealth; I am your hoard.'"

Children

1. 'Ali said, "Having a small family is one of two kinds of ease."

2. Lao-tzu said, "People are supple when they are born, and rigid when they die. All beings, even plants and trees, are tender when born and brittle when they die. So rigidity is the associate of death, flexibility is the associate of life."

4. The Huainan Masters said, "Those who know the source of law and order change to adapt to the times. Those who do not know the source of law and order change with customs. Manners and duties change with customs. Pedants make it their business to follow precedent, preserving the old based on convention, thinking that government is otherwise impossible. This is like trying to put a square peg in a round hole."

Wen-tzu said, "Different ages have different concerns; when times change, customs change. Laws are set up in consideration of the age, works are undertaken according to the time. The laws and measures of ancient rulers were dissimilar, not because they purposely contradicted one another, but because the tasks of their times were different. Therefore they did not take established laws for rules, but took for their rules the reasons why laws were laws, progressively changing along with the development of civilization."

5. 'Ali said, "You are getting enough from your intelligence if it makes plain to you the ways that lead you astray from your integrity."

6. 'Ali said, "Hearts are in fact desirous, preoccupied, and flighty; so approach them by way of their desires and their preoccupations, for the heart goes blind when it is coerced."

Politicians and Philosophers

1. The Huainan Masters said, "The ruler is the mind of the nation. When the mind is orderly, all nodes are calm; when the mind is disturbed, all nodes are deranged."

   The Huainan Masters also said, "To indulge the perversities of an individual, thereby increasing troubles throughout the land, is unacceptable to natural reason."

2. The Huainan Masters said, "When political leaders ruin their countries and wreck their lands, themselves to die at others' hands, a laughingstock of all the world, it is always because of their desires."

3. The Huainan Masters said, "With the art of the Way it is not possible to seek fame through promotion, but it is possible to develop oneself by retirement. It is not possible to gain advantages by it, but it is possible to avoid injuries."

   'Ali said, "Is there no free individual who will leave this unswallowed morsel to those who are attached to it? There is no price for your selves but Paradise, so do not sell them for anything else."

4. The Huainan Masters said, "Sages do not need authority to be noble, do not need wealth to be rich, and do not need power to be strong. Peaceful and empty, they are not subject to outside influences."

5. The Huainan Masters said, "Greedy leaders and harsh rulers oppress their subjects and bleed their people to satisfy their own interminable desires. Thus the commoners have no way to benefit from the harmony of heaven or walk upon the blessings of earth."

7. The Huainan Masters said, "The military operations of effective leaders are considered philosophically, planned strategically, and supported justly. They are not intended to destroy what exists, but to preserve what is perishing."

'Ali said, "Whoever hurries with the reins of his expectation stumbles because of it."

8. The Huainan Masters said, "Those who used arms in ancient times did not do so to expand their territory or obtain wealth. They did so for the survival and continuity of nations on the brink of destruction and extinction, to settle disorder in the world, and to get rid of what harmed the common people."

The Huainan Masters also said, "Sages' use of arms is like combing hair or thinning sprouts: a few are removed for the benefit of many. There is no harm greater than killing innocent people and supporting unjust rulers. There is no calamity worse than exhausting the world's resources to provide for the desires of an individual."

The Huainan Masters also said, "Those who make war to gain lands cannot fully become kings of those lands, and those

who make war in their own interests cannot make their ac-
complishments stand."

'Ali said, "Pardon is the tax on victory."

'Ali also said, "When you have overpowered an enemy,
show him forgiveness out of gratitude for the ability to overpower him."

9. The Huainan Masters said, "Enlightened people are able to
criticize rulers when they see a fault, because they are mindless of reprisal. They are able to defer to the wise when they
see them, because they are mindless of social status."

Wisdom

1. Confucius said to a pupil, "Do you think I have come to know
many things by studying them?" The pupil answered, "Yes,
isn't it so?" Confucius said, "No. I penetrate them by their un-
derlying unity."

   Lao-tzu said, "There is something undifferentiated prior to
the origin of sky and earth; inaccessible, utterly silent, independent and unchanging; it can be considered the matrix of
the universe."

2. 'Ali said, "I wonder at the one who doubts God even though
he sees God's creation."

   'Ali also said, "I know God the Glorified by the nullifica-
tion of resolutions, the unraveling of arrangements, and the
invalidation of intentions."

3. Confucius said, "Be an exemplary man of learning, not a trivial
pedant."

4. 'Ali said, "Meditation is a clear mirror."

7. The Huainan Masters said, "Sages emulate Heaven and go
along with its conditions."

9. A Buddhist proverb says, "My parents gave birth to me, but my companions raised me."

10. 'Ali said, "Knowledge is better than wealth. Knowledge protects you, while you protect wealth. Wealth is diminished by spending, while knowledge grows by use."

11. 'Ali said, "Know with certain knowledge that God does not grant any mortal—no matter how great his strategy, no matter how intense his seeking, and no matter how powerful his machinations—more than what is determined in the Recollection of Wisdom."

Change

1. 'Ali said, "Destiny is two days; one for you and one against you. So when it is for you, do not be proud or reckless; and when it is against you, then be patient."

   The Huainan Masters said, "Sages cannot cause calamity not to come, but they trust themselves not to beckon it. They cannot ensure that fortune will come, but they trust themselves not to repel it. When calamity occurs, it is not that they have sought that whereby it arises; so even in extremity they are not troubled. When fortune occurs, it is not that they have sought that whereby it comes about; so even in success they are not proud."

   'Ali said, "Through changes in circumstances the essence of individuals is known."

3. 'Ali said, "I wonder at the proud one, who was a drop of sperm yesterday and will be a rotting corpse tomorrow."

   'Ali also said, "So many entertain hopes of what they do not attain, build houses they do not live in, and amass that which they are going to leave behind them."

The Human Soul

1. Zen Master Bankei said, "Hating people or being jealous of them is the condition of hell; anger and rage is the condition of demonia; covetous thoughts full of greed and stinginess are the condition of ghouls. Regretting afterward and longing for what's ahead is folly, the condition of animals. . . . While born in the honorable human state, taking the quality of clarity which discerns good and bad, right and wrong, and turning it into something worthless, is a miserable, pitiful thing."

   Confucius said, "You are worthy of the name *human* if you can practice five things in this world: respectfulness, magnanimity, truthfulness, acuity, and generosity."

2. The Taoist adept Liu I-ming wrote, "The reason why people's minds are not clear and their natures are not stable is that they are full of craving and emotion. Add to this eons of mental habit, acquired influences deluding the mind, their outgrowths clogging up the opening of awareness—this is like water being murky, like a mirror being dusty. The original true mind and true essence are totally lost. The feelings and senses are unruly, subject to all kinds of influences, taking in all sorts of things, defiling the mind."

3. The Huainan Masters said, "When the mind neither sorrows nor delights, that is supreme attainment of virtue."

   A Buddhist proverb says, "When you recognize the essence of mind in the midst of the flow, there is no joy, and no sorrow."

4. 'Ali said, "Physical health comes from having little envy."

5 and 6. Confucius said, "Cultivated people have three disciplines. When they are young and their physical energy is not yet stabilized, they are disciplined in matters of sexuality. When they mature and their physical energy is at the peak of

strength, they are disciplined in matters of convention. When they are old and their physical energy is in decline, they are disciplined in matters of gain."

The Huainan Masters said, "The eyes, ears, and palate do not know what to take and what to leave; when the mind governs them, they each find their proper place. Seen from this point of view, it is evident that desire cannot be overcome; yet it can be done to the point where insanity does not occur, by any who master themselves and develop their nature, regulate sexual activity and moderate their dining, make their emotions gentle, and act and rest appropriately."

7. The Huainan Masters said, "The harmonious joyfulness and peaceful calm of ancient sages were their nature."

8. The Huainan Masters said, "What sages learn is to return their nature to the beginning and let the mind travel freely in openness. What developed people learn is to link their nature to vast emptiness and become aware of the silent infinite."

Law

1. The Huainan Masters said, "The eyes are fond of color and form, the ears are fond of voice and sound, the palate is fond of flavor: what enjoys contacts without cognizance of their profit and harm is greed. When you eat what doesn't settle in the stomach, what you listen to does not accord with the Way, and what you look at is unsuited to nature, there are battles at these three points of interaction: what uses duty to assert mastery is mind."

Lao-tzu said, "When the courts are very tidy but the fields are very weedy and the granaries are very empty, to wear colorful clothing and carry sharp swords, to eat to satiation and possess excess wealth, is called the arrogance of thieves."

Muhammad the Prophet said, "A believer eats in one gut, while a disbeliever or a hypocrite eats in seven guts."

'Ali said, "Justice puts things in their places, while generosity takes them out of their domains."

Confucius said of a student who was sleeping in the daytime, "Rotten wood cannot be sculpted, a manure wall cannot be plastered."

'Ali said, "How sleep demolishes the resolutions of the day!"

Lao-tzu said, "The sage avoids the extreme, avoids the grandiose, avoids the extravagant."

2. Lao-tzu said, "Wise people wear rough clothing, concealing a treasure."

Confucius said, "A man who aspires to the Way yet is ashamed of poor clothing and poor food is not worth talking to."

3. Muhammad the Prophet said, "The example of one who observes the ordinances of God and one who disparages them is as that of people who draw lots for places on a ship, and some got the higher places while others got the lower places. Whenever those in the lower places wanted to get water to drink, they made their way past those who were above them. So they said, 'Let us make a hole in our part of the ship, so that we will not trouble those above us.' Now then, if the others let them do what they wanted, it would destroy them all. But if they prevented them from doing so, they would save themselves, and would save everyone."

4. Wen-tzu said, "When human leaders determine laws, they should first apply them to themselves, to test and prove them. If a regulation works on the rulers themselves, then it may be enjoined upon the populace. Laws are the plumb lines of the

land, the measures used by human leaders, the established rules regulating the unruly."

Self-Destruction

1 and 2. 'Ali said, "Greed motivates without producing, and guarantees without fulfilling. Many a drinker of water chokes before his thirst is quenched, and the greater the importance of that for which one vies, the greater the calamity of losing it. Longing blinds the eye of insight, and good luck comes to the one who does not come after it."

Wen-tzu said, "There are three kinds of death that are not natural passing away. If you drink and eat immoderately and treat the body carelessly and cheaply, then illnesses will kill you. If you are endlessly greedy and ambitious, then penalties will kill you. If you allow small groups to infringe upon the rights of large masses, and allow the weak to be oppressed by the strong, then weapons will kill you."

3. Lao-tzu said, "Sages want not to want."

4. A Buddhist proverb says, "Bring in a wolf, and it'll crap in the house."

Modesty

1. Lao-tzu said, "Great skillfulness appears clumsy, great surplus is kept out of sight."

Huanchu Daoren wrote, "To boast of one's work or show off one's literary accomplishment is to base one's person on external things."

'Ali said, "How many have been lured into destruction by being well treated, have been misled by being protected, have been seduced by being well spoken of!"

2. 'Ali said, "People oppose what they are ignorant about."

'Ali also said, "Whoever habitually engages in disputation will not see the dawn of his night."

3. 'Ali said, "We are assistants of fate, and our selves are a target of death. So where can you expect permanence when the night and the day do not promote anything without soon turning around and attacking and destroying what they have built, scattering what they have brought together?"

5. 'Ali said, "Whoever gives up saying 'I don't know' has been mortally stricken."

6. Confucius said, "Shall I teach you how to know something? Realize you know it when you know it, and realize you don't know it when you don't."

Lao-tzu said, "It is excellent to know innocently; it is sick to feign knowledge ignorantly."

Virtue and Action

1. 'Ali said, "Faith is experience by the heart, avowal by the tongue, and action by the limbs."

2. 'Ali said, "Generosity is that which comes from one's own initiative; as for what is given in response to a request, that is either shame or rebuke."

3. Liu I-ming said, "If you cannot even accumulate virtues, how can you presume to imagine realization of the Way?"

The Huainan Masters said, "There are three dangers in the world. To have many privileges but few virtues is the first danger. To be high in rank but low on ability is the second danger. To receive a large salary without personally accomplishing much is the third danger."

Huanchu Daoren wrote, "Virtue is the master of talent, talent is the servant of virtue. Talent without virtue is like a house where there is no master and the servant manages affairs. How can there be no mischief?"

7. Confucius said, "I have never seen anyone who was firm." Someone named a certain disciple. Confucius said, "He is covetous—how can he be firm?"

'Ali said, "The greedy one is in the shackles of abasement." He also said, "Whoever is full of greed debases himself."

9. 'Ali said, "Understand information you hear with the reasoning of responsibility, not the reasoning of the reporter; for there are many reports of knowledge, but few are responsible."

10. 'Ali said, "Be generous without squandering, appreciate value without being stingy."

Appearance and Reality

1, 2, and 3. 'Ali said, "For those who make their inner thoughts wholesome, God will make their outward manifestations wholesome."

3. 'Ali said, "These hearts weary as the bodies weary, so seek for them rarities of wisdom."

4. 'Ali said, "O God, I take refuge with You from appearing to the public to be better than I am, while my inner mind is repulsive to You for what it conceals."

5. 'Ali said, "There are servants of God whom God favors with blessings for the service of others, and whom God keeps supplied as long as they are generous with what they have." He also said, "Generosity awakens affection more than kinship does."

7. Muhammad the Prophet said, "One who recites the Qur'an is like a citron, whose flavor is good and whose scent is good. One who does not recite the Qur'an is like a date, whose fla-

vor is good but which has no scent. An immoral person who
recites the Qur'an is like basil, whose scent is good but whose
taste is bitter. An immoral person who does not recite the
Qur'an is like the colocynth, whose taste is bitter and which
has no scent."

Knowledge and Ignorance

1. 'Ali said, "There is no wealth like intelligence, and no poverty
like ignorance." He also said, "You will find the ignorant either remiss or excessive."

6. 'Ali said, "Wisdom stammers in the heart of a hypocrite, until
it leaves and comes to rest by its like in the heart of a believer."

Zen Master Fushan said, "The case of those who, while
their study has not yet arrived at the Way, still flash their
learning and run off at the mouth with intellectual understanding, using eloquence and sharpness of tongue to gain victories, is like outhouses painted vermilion—it only increases
the odor."

7. Once Lord Chi Heng was reading a book, when a craftsman
said to him, "May I ask what you are reading, sir?" The lord
said, "A book of the sages." The craftsman asked, "Are the
sages alive?" The lord said, "They are dead." The craftsman remarked, "Then what you are reading is the dregs of the ancients."

Zen Master Huang-po said to a group, "You are all slurping
dregs. If you go on like this, where will you have *today*?"

Negativity

1. The I Ching says, "Cultivated people eliminate wrath and cupidity."

Confucius said, "Petty people are always fretting."

2. 'Ali said, "The greatest wealth is unconcern with people's possessions." He also said, "One who is satisfied with the sustenance God grants him does not grieve over what he has missed."

3. 'Ali said, "Rage is a kind of madness, because the sufferer is regretful; so if he is not regretful, that means his madness is ingrained."

6. 'Ali said, "One who cautions you is as one who brings you good news."

9. Confucius said, "Cultivated people reach upward; petty people reach downward." He also said, "Cultivated people foster what is good in others, not what is bad. Petty people do the opposite."

10. Muhammad the Prophet said, "Good companions and bad companions are like sellers of musk and the furnace of the smithy. You lose nothing from the musk seller, whether you buy some, or smell, or are imbued with its fragrance. The furnace of the smithy, on the other hand, burns your house and your clothes, or you get a noxious odor."

12. 'Ali said, "Words are under your control until you have spoken them; but you come under their control once you have spoken them." He also said, "The heart of the fool is in his mouth."

15. Huanchu Daoren wrote, "Observe people with cool eyes, listen to their words with cool ears. Confront feelings with cool emotions, reflect on principles with a cool mind."

15 and 16. Huanchu Daoren wrote, "When you hear of bad people, don't despise them right away, for their bad repute might be the sputterings of cavilers. When you hear of good people, don't rush to befriend them, because their good repute might have been made up by dishonest people trying to get ahead."

17. 'Ali said, "Forbearance and patience are consonant one with the other; loftiness of aspiration produces them both."

19. Ali said, "Anyone who wishes to keep his dignity should give up disputation."

20. The Huainan Masters said, "Praise may cause people trouble; criticism may help them."

Realism

1. 'Ali said, "One who would not receive something anyway would not get it by contrivance." He also said, "Put aside your pride, set down your arrogance, and remember your grave."

2. The *I Ching* says, "Accept others with tolerance, be positive and farsighted in your endeavors, and you can be impartial and balanced in action."

3 and 4. The Master of Demon Valley said, "Those who speak without seeing what type of person they are talking to will be opposed, and those who speak without finding out the state of mind of the person they are talking to will be denied."

Pleasure

1. The Huainan Masters said, "Those in whom sense overpowers desire flourish, while those in whom desire overpowers sense perish." They also said, "Habitual desires deplete people's energy; likes and dislikes strain people's minds."

2. 'Ali said, "Truth is weighty but wholesome; falsehood is light but poisonous."

3. Ali said, "How sleep demolishes the resolutions of the day!"

5. The Huainan Masters said, "The eyes are fond of color and form, the ears are fond of voice and sound, the palate is fond

of flavor: what enjoys contacts without cognizance of their profit and harm is greed."

Family and Friends

1. Huanchu Daoren wrote, "There is a true Buddha in family life; there is a real Tao in everyday activities. If people can be sincere and harmonious, promoting communication with a cheerful demeanor and friendly words, that is much better than formal meditation practice."

3. Ali said, "Kinship is more in need of friendship than is friendship in need of kinship."

Mind and Matter

1. The Huainan Masters said, "If you set your mind free in tranquillity and relinquish your body in leisure, thereby to await the direction of nature, spontaneously happy within and free from hurry without, even the magnitude of the universe cannot change you at all; even should the sun and moon be eclipsed, that does not dampen your will. Then you are as if noble even if lowly, and you are as if rich even if poor."

Wen-tzu said, "Those who practiced the Way in ancient times ordered their feelings and nature and governed their mental functions, nurturing them with harmony and keeping them in porportion. Enjoying the Way, they forgot about lowliness; secure in virtue, they forgot about poverty."

2. Wen-tzu said, "Consider the world light, and the spirit is not burdened; consider myriad things slight, and the mind is not confused. Consider life and death equal, and the intellect is not afraid; consider change as sameness, and clarity is not obscured. . . . Those who act justly can be pressed by humanitarianism but cannot be threatened by arms; they can be corrected by righteousness but cannot be hooked by profit.

Ideal people will die for justice and cannot be stayed by riches and rank. Those who act justly cannot be intimidated by death."

3. Wen-tzu said, "[Those who practiced the Way in ancient times] considered the world extra and did not try to possess it; they left everyone and everything to themselves and did not seek profit. How could they lose their essential life because of poverty or riches, high or low status?"

4. Wen-tzu said, "The physical body may pass away, but the spirit does not change. Use the unchanging to respond to changes, and there is never any limit. What changes returns to formlessness, while that which does not change lives together with the universe. So what gives birth to life is not itself born; what it gives birth to is what is born. What produces change does not itself change; what it changes is what changes. This is where real people roam, the path of quintessence."

5. The Huainan Masters said, "The vital spirit belongs to heaven, the physical body belongs to earth. When the vital spirit goes home and the physical body returns to its origin, then where is the self?"

6. Wen-tzu said, "The body is the house of life; energy is the basis of life; spirit is the controller of life: if one of these loses its position, all three are injured. Therefore when the spirit is in the lead, the body follows it, with beneficial results; when the body is in the lead, the spirit follows it, with harmful results. Those people whose lives are gluttony and lust are tripped and blinded by power and profit, seduced and charmed by fame and status."

7. 'Ali said, "God has a right in every blessing, and whoever discharges that is given more from it, and whoever shorts that right is in danger of losing the blessing."

8. 'Ali said, "There is no wealth like intelligence."

10. Wen-tzu said, "The physical body may pass away, but the spirit does not change."

Friends and Enemies

1. Ali said, "Understanding is what makes relationships."

2. 'Ali said, "How many have been lured into destruction by being well treated, have been misled by being protected, have been seduced by being well spoken of!"

3. Zen Master Yuan-wu said, "In trying to distinguish good people from bad, if you dislike it when they say you are wrong and like it when they follow you, then good and bad cannot be distinguished. Only the wise do not dislike to hear how they are wrong and do not delight in having others go along with them."

4. Zen master Kuei-shan wrote, "Familiarity with the evil increases wrong knowledge and views, day and night creating evil."

5, 6, and 7. Huanchu Daoren wrote, "Flatterers and fawners are like a draft that gets into the flesh; one is harmed unawares."

7. When people praised him to his face, 'Ali said, "O God, You know me better than I do myself, and I know myself better than they do. O God, make us better than they think we are, and forgive us what they do not know."

8 and 9. 'Ali said, "The biggest failures are those who have failed to win friends; but even bigger failures are those who lose what friends they have made." He also said, "One who follows the slanderer loses true friends." He also said, "Friendship is a profitable relationship; and do not trust the disaffected."

10. Asked how he overcame his opponents, 'Ali said, "I never met any man who did not help me against himself."

12. Huanchu Daoren wrote, "When fate slights me in terms of prosperity, I respond by enriching my virtue. When fate belabors me physically, I make up for it by making my mind free. When fate obstructs me by circumstances, I get through by elevating my way of life. What can fate do to me?" He also said, "In adversity, everything that surrounds you is a kind of medicine that helps you refine your conduct."

13. 'Ali said, "Justice is fairness, and goodness is kindness."

14. 'Ali said, "Do not associate with a fool, because he presents his behavior in a favorable light and wishes you would be like him." He also said, "Do not befriend a fool, for he hurts you when he wants to help you. And do not befriend a stingy man, for he will distance himself from you when he is most needed. And do not befriend a profligate, as he will sell you for a trifle. And do not befriend a liar, for he is like a mirage, making the distant seem near to you and the near seem distant."

15. 'Ali said, "Whoever extends wishful thinking spoils action."

16. 'Ali said, "A man's vanity is one of the things that inhibit his intelligence."

Justice

1. Confucius said, "If you would be employed by a just country, it is shameful to be employed by an unjust country." He also said, "Exemplary people understand matters of justice; small people understand matters of profit."

3. The Huainan Masters said, "Humanity and justice are the warp and woof of society; this never changes. If people can assess their abilities and take the time to examine what they do, then even if changes take place daily, that is all right." They also said, "What enables a nation to survive is humanity and justice; what enables people to live is practical virtue. A nation

without justice will perish even if it is large; people without good will will be wounded even if they are brave."

4. Huanchu Daoren wrote, "Don't be too severe in criticizing people's faults; consider how much they can bear."

Self-Government

1. Zen Master Fo-chih said, "A swift horse can run fast, but does not dare gallop freely because of the bit and halter. When petty people, while obstinate and belligerent, do not indulge their feelings, it is because of punishments and laws. When the flow of consciousness does not dare to cling to objects, this is the power of awareness. If people have no awareness and are unreflective, they are like fast horses with no bit and bridle."

The Huainan Masters said, "When your spirit rules, your body benefits from obedience to it; when your body is in control, your spirit is harmed by obedience to it."

2. The Huainan Masters said, "Habitual desires deplete people's energy; likes and dislikes strain people's minds. If you don't get rid of them quickly, your will and energy will diminish day by day."

3. Huanchu Daoren said, "When anger or passion boils up, even when we are clearly aware we still go ahead. Who is it that goes ahead? If we can turn our thoughts around in this way, the devil becomes the conscience."

4. The Huainan Masters said, "If you know the vastness of the universe, you cannot be oppressed by death or life. . . . If you know the happiness of the unborn state, you cannot be frightened by death."

5. Zen Master Ming-chiao said, "The study of saints and sages is certainly not fulfilled in one day. When there is not enough

time during the day, continue into the night; accumulate it over the months and years, and it will naturally develop."

6. 'Ali said, "Whoever lets his tongue rule him becomes despicable in his own eyes." He also said, "The heart of the fool is in his mouth, while the tongue of the intelligent man is in his heart."

9. 'Ali said, "Time wears out bodies even as it renews hopes; it brings death nearer and removes aspiration. Whoever takes advantage of it becomes exhausted; whoever lets it slip by toils." He also said, "What a difference there is between two actions: an act whose pleasure departs but whose consequence remains, and an act whose difficulty departs but whose reward remains."

10. The Master of Demon Valley wrote, "The mouth is the door of the mind; the mind is the host of the spirit. Will, intention, joy, desire, thought, worry, knowledge, and planning all go in and out through the door. Therefore they are governed by opening and closing, controlled in their exit and entry"

12. A Zen proverb says, "Once a word enters the public domain, nine horses cannot drag it back."

13. 'Ali said, "This world of yours is more worthless in my eyes than pig entrails in the hand of a leper."

14. 'Ali said, "Endure with the patience of the free, or else forget with the forgetfulness of the ingenuous."

15. 'Ali said, "Do not ask about what does not exist, for there is work for you in what does exist."

16. Huanchu Daoren wrote, "The way to transcend the world is right in the midst of involvement with the world; it is not necessary to cut off human relations to escape society."

18. 'Ali said, "No wealth brings greater return than intelligence. . . .

There is no intelligence like good planning, and no high-mindedness like conscience in awe of Truth."

The Life of the World

1. 'Ali said, "One who expects death hastens to good deeds."

2. 'Ali said, "Greed is endless slavery."

4. 'Ali said, "Each breath one takes is a step toward one's destiny." He also said, "The departure is imminent."

5. The Huainan Masters said, "Sages have within them the means to contact higher potential; they do not lose their self-mastery on account of high or low status, poverty or wealth, toil or leisure."

   'Ali said, "One who is aggrieved at the world is discontent with the judgment of God, and one who complains about misfortunes that befall him is complaining about his Lord."

Spiritual Perception

2. This allegory attributed to Pythagoras is analogous to the Sufi theme of the King's Son, an archetypal allegory of life in the world as spiritual exile from which the soul can be awakened to seek to return to its origin.

3. Zen Master Tung-shan said, "There is one thing, which supports heaven and earth. It is absolutely black. It is always in the midst of activity, yet activity cannot contain it."

5. 'Ali was asked, "How can God call all creatures to account without being seen by them?" He replied, "Just as God sustains them without being seen by them."

6. The Qur'an says, "No vision can comprehend God, but God comprehends all vision. And God is most subtle, perfectly aware."

Political Science

1. Wen-tzu said, "When rulers are wise, they guide and judge fairly; wise and good people are in office, skilled and capable people are at work. Wealth is distributed downward, and all the people are aware of their blessings. When they degenerate, cliques and factions each promote their cronies, discarding public interest for private. With outsiders and insiders overthrowing each other, the positions of power are occupied by the wily and treacherous, while the good and wise remain hidden."

2. 'Ali said, "Whoever sets himself up as a leader of other people should start educating himself before educating others, and let him teach by his conduct before teaching by his tongue."

3. According to the Huainan Masters, a lord asked one of his ministers what made a nation perish. The minister replied, "Numerous victories in numerous wars." The lord said, "A nation is fortunate to win numerous victories in numerous wars—why would it perish thereby?" The minister replied, "When there are repeated wars, the people are weakened; when they score repeated victories, rulers become haughty. Let haughty rulers command weakened people, and rare is the nation that will not perish as a result."

   The Huainan Masters said, "If you indulge desires so much as to lose your essential nature, nothing you do is ever right: to train yourself in this way leads to danger; to govern a nation in this way leads to chaos; to take up arms in this way leads to defeat."

4. The Huainan Masters said, "When the directives of the leadership are ignored because of factionalism, laws are broken out of treachery, intellectuals busy themselves fabricating clever deceits, mettlesome men occupy themselves fighting, admin-

istrators monopolize authority, petty bureaucrats hold power, and cliques curry favor to manipulate the leadership. Then, even though the nation may seem to exist, the ancients would have said it has perished."

The Huainan Masters also said, "When the territory is large because of virtue and the leadership is honored because of virtue, that is best. When the territory is large because of justice and the leadership is honored because of justice, that is next best. When the territory is large because of strength and the leadership is honored because of strength, that is lowest."

6. The Huainan Masters said, "The customs of a decadent society use cunning and deceit to dress up the useless."

8. The Master of Demon Valley said, "When you apprehend people's feelings and states of mind, then you can use your arts masterfully. Applying this method, you can put people off and can bring them in; you can form ties with people, and can separate yourself from them. Therefore, when sages set things up, they use this means to get to know people beforehand and establish solidarity with them. Based on reason, virtue, humanity, justice, courtesy, and culture, they figure out plans."

11. 'Ali said, "When you have overpowered an enemy, show him forgiveness out of gratitude for the ability to overpower him." He also said, "The foremost of people in forgiveness is the most powerful of them in punishment."

12. The Master of the Hidden Storehouse said, "When trust is complete, the world is secure. When trust is lost, the world is dangerous. When the common people labor diligently and yet their money and goods run out, then contentious and antagonistic attitudes arise, and people do not trust each other. When people do not trust each other, this is due to unfairness in government practices. When there is unfairness in government practices, this is the fault of officials. When officials are

at fault, penalties and rewards are unequal. When penalties and rewards are unequal, this means the leadership is not conscientious."

13. The Huainan Masters said, "The behavior of sage kings did not hurt the feelings of the people, so even while the kings enjoyed themselves the world was at peace. The evil kings denied the truthful and declared them outlaws, so as the kings enjoyed themselves everything went to ruin."

Speech and Silence

1 and 3. 'Ali said, "Guard your tongue as you guard your gold, for many a word snatches away blessings and brings adversity."

3. The Master of Demon Valley said, "Opening up is to assess people's feelings; shutting down is to make sure of their sincerity."

4. 'Ali said, "Do not say what you do not know, but neither say all of what you do know."

5. Lao-tzu said, "Truthful words are not prettified, prettified words are not truthful." He also said, "Blowhards cannot stand."

Education

1 and 2. Confucius said, "Be an exemplary man of learning, not a trivial pedant."

8. Buddha said, "Whatever knowledge a fool acquires tends to be harmful; it destroys the fool's virtue, going to his head."

Select Bibliography

Glubb, Sir John. *A Short History of the Arab Peoples*. New York: Barnes and Noble, 1995.

Gutas, Dimitri. *Greek Wisdom Literature in Arabic Translation: A Study of the Graeco-Arabic Gnomologia*. New Haven: American Oriental Society, 1975.

Lewis, Bernard. *The Arabs in History*. New York: Harper & Row, 1960.

Maimonides, Moses. *The Guide for the Perplexed*. Translated by M. Friedlander. New York: Dover Publications, 1956.

Maimonides, Obadyah. *The Treatise of the Pool*. Translated by Paul Fenton. London: Octagon Press, 1981.

Palmer, Louis. *Adventures in Afghanistan*. London: Octagon Press, 1990.

Rosenthal, Franz. *Greek Philosophy in the Arab World*. Hampshire, England: Variorum, 1990.

Select Bibliography _____

Scott, Ernest. *The People of the Secret.* London: Octagon Press, 1983.

Shah, Idries. *The Sufis.* New York: Doubleday, 1964.

Shah, Ikbal Ali. "Sufism and the Indian Philosophies," in *Sufi Thought and Action.* Assembled by Idries Shah. London: Octagon Press, 1990.

Waddell, Helen. The Wandering Scholars. New York, Doubleday, 1955.